A PORTFOLIO OF

STORAGE
IDEAS

CONTENTS

© Copyright 1996
Cy DeCosse Incorporated
5900 Green Oak Drive
Minnetonka, Minnesota 55343
1-800-328-3895
All rights reserved

Library of Congress
Cataloging-in-Publication Data
Portfolio of storage ideas.
p. cm.
ISBN 0-86573-964-1 (softcover)
1. Storage in the home.
I. Cy DeCosse Incorporated.
TX309.P67 1996
648'.8—dc20
96-1754   CIP

Author: Home How-To Institute™
Creative Director: William B. Jones
Associate Creative Director: Tim Himsel
Group Executive Editor: Paul Currie
Managing Editor: Carol Harvatin
Editor: Mark Biscan
Art Director: Ruth Eischens
Copy Editor: Janice Cauley
Vice President of Development
    Planning & Production: Jim Bindas
Production Coordinator: Laura Hokkanen

Printed on American paper by Webcrafters Inc. (0596)

CY DECOSSE INCORPORATED

A Cowles Magazines Company

Chairman/CEO: Bruce Barnet
Chairman Emeritus: Cy DeCosse
President & Chief Operating Officer: Nino Tarantino
Editor-in-Chief: William B. Jones

99 98 97 96 / 5 4 3 2 1

Photos on these two pages courtesy of California Closets,
ClosetMaid®, Crystal Cabinet Works Inc., Cy DeCosse Inc.,
Grange, KraftMaid Cabinetry Inc. and Stanley Home Decor

WHAT MAKES GREAT STORAGE?

Our quest for storage evolved from our desires for material things and a need to archive our lives. What we store is determined by what we need, what we accumulate and how we keep it. Today we have more to store than ever before. And we are concerned about the value of our belongings, so we want a place to put them that will also protect them.

Successful storage goes hand-in-hand with organization. Organized storage means being able to easily retrieve stored items wherever they may be, whenever you need them. It also means being able to see, access and retrieve items easily. This is why you need to think as much about efficiency as capacity when planning your storage. Too much time spent straightening and looking for things means your time isn't being used efficiently.

Storage options can be defined by the function or functions of the storage unit. For example, an open storage unit has open shelves or cubbyholes, while a pull-out unit has components that pull out, like drawers, doors or shelves. Every storage unit can be categorized into one or more types of storage. It is common for a storage unit to be classified as more

than one specific type of storage. They are often a combination of different types. For example, a bookcase can be freestanding, as well as adjustable and open storage.

The type of storage and features you choose will depend on the function you wish the unit to perform. *A Portfolio of Storage Ideas* examines the distinctions between the different types of storage, and takes a look at how each can be applied to various storage situations around the house. You'll find a variety of effective storage systems, from adjustable to customized, that will inspire you, as well as ideas on how to get maximum efficiency from your space. *A Portfolio of Storage Ideas* will help you create a storage system that works best for you.

You'll also find examples of incredible specialized storage created for the specific storage needs of items such as food and wine or electronic items. The second half of the book features a portfolio section of storage ideas for each room of the house. Here you'll find inspired examples of the various types of storage tied together to create innovative and highly effective storage space.

This librarylike bookcase accommodates a variety of storage needs. Uniquely styled with rounded corner pieces, this unit includes a space for a home theater, pull-out drawers and lots of open, adjustable shelves.

Good organization is half the battle when it comes to effective storage. This capable closet is organized for efficiency. Double-hung rods hold twice as much clothing. Cubby compartments keep shoes and folded items orderly. And the space at the top of the closet is utilized by adding two rows of open shelving. Here, blankets, linens and an assortment of plastic storage containers are organized and out of sight, yet easily accessible.

*A **multistorage pantry** makes a distinct difference in storage and organization for this kitchen. Swing-out doors and open shelves maximize storage space and make all items easy to see and easy to access.*

Planning

SUCCESSFUL STORAGE STRATEGIES

One of the primary goals of successful storage and space utilization is to maintain the illusion of spaciousness. By improving your current storage system you can enjoy a more functional, pleasant-looking home, as well as save time and reduce stress. Successful storage is knowing what to store, and how to store it. The only wrong way to organize your storage is to make it too complicated.

Different types of storage can be classified by the way they function—adjustable, built-to-fit, open, pull-out and freestanding storage, to name a few. When comparing these different types of storage systems to one another you'll discover as many similarities as differences. For example, an entertainment center with cabinets for storing electronic components and open bookshelves includes closed storage, open storage, display storage and even freestanding storage, if the unit is indeed standing on its own. Even though there are similarities among the different storage types, each has characteristics distinctive to that type of storage. The trick to successful storage is deciding

which type makes the most efficient use of your existing storage space and unique storage needs.

The right type, or combination of types, of storage can add space and a certain style to a room. The most effective storage systems maximize your storage capacity without using any more existing space. Lifestyle, architectural style, existing decor and budget are the primary factors that will affect which type of storage, or combination of storage systems, will work best in your home.

Many effective storage systems combine different types of storage. For example, a wall unit or entertainment center is most efficient and effective for storage when it includes a combination of open and closed storage. The most common types of storage systems are adjustable, open, freestanding, built-to-fit, stationary, pull-out, customized and item-specific. The way you decide to arrange and retrieve stored items will determine the type of storage that will work best for you.

The multifunctional design *makes this modern wall unit a storage masterpiece. It includes an abundance of sturdy, fixed shelving that is ideal for storing heavy items like books. The open shelves act as display cases for an interesting array of art objects. This storage system also includes a number of pull-out drawers and a cabinet with a hide-away folding door for the television and other electronic equipment.*

SUCCESSFUL STORAGE STRATEGIES

You'll find that in many instances more than one type of storage system can be used to store similar items. The system you choose will depend on your existing available space, personal preferences and individual lifestyle.

An open storage system is a good choice for items like books, CDs, videos, shoes, hats and folded items. Pull-out storage systems work well for organizing items like silverware, cosmetics, jewelry and pantry items, such as canned or dry goods. Freestanding storage systems can be flexible and functional. A coffee table with cabinets and drawers, a man's valet or a rolling kitchen cart with a butcher block top are all excellent examples of freestanding storage.

Investigate each type of storage system to determine what will work best for you. You may even want to come up with your own alternative uses for each type of storage system. For example, item-specific storage can be used to store alternative items as well. A tie rack can also be used to store scarves or necklaces, shoe pockets be used to hold lingerie or gloves and belt racks can serve as hooks for clothing, necklaces or ties.

Under-the-counter storage that pulls out, *then swings open, is ideal for accessing deep cabinets where cumbersome items like pots and pans are often stored.*

(above) **Adjustable shelving** lets you reconfigure your storage for every situation. The open, vinyl-coated wire shelves allow you to see every item for easy inventory.
(right) **Adjustable shelves** increase the storage options in this narrow linen closet.

An organized closet helps you avoid early morning madness. Grouping items by function, hierarchy of use or simply by color puts anything you're looking for at your fingertips.

Planning

ORGANIZING YOUR EXISTING STORAGE

Begin organizing your storage space by sorting out items that you and your family use now, or will definitely use in the near future. Get rid of anything that doesn't fit into one of these categories and begin to develop a storage system that is well organized and easily accessible to store the rest. The system of organization you create should be based on what works for you.

One way to organize is by hierarchy of use. In this system items are stored by frequency of use and ease of accessibility. The first step to this type of organization is to group seldom-used or seasonal items together. Even though they are seldom used, you should be able to get to these items easily when the time comes. Marking the boxes with their contents and using file cabinets are simple ways to make stored items easy to access.

Classifying items as active or inactive storage is another way to organize your system. Active storage is for items you use or wear every day. This includes anything you might need or wear at least once a month, as well as items like linens, often-used tools or utensils, household records or sporting equipment. Anything you use less frequently, such as lawn furniture, or things you use or wear only once or twice a year belongs in inactive storage. Remember, inactive storage doesn't mean hard to reach; it still must be organized and easily accessible.

Active storage areas include drawers and shelves that are within arm's reach or at eye level: countertops, hooks on doors, the center of cabinet shelves and closet poles. Inactive storage spaces include drawers or shelves that are beyond arm's reach or above eye level, floor-level drawers (except in a child's room, where this would be active storage), sealed boxes, unused trunks or suitcases, the blind sides of cabinet shelves or a loft in a garage, attic or cellar.

(above and left) **Transform your closet from confusion and chaos**—to clean and well kept, with an intelligently organized storage system. Take a look at this closet after it was reorganized with a well-planned storage system—shirts are with shirts, dresses are together, sweaters hang neatly at eye level and shoes, tucked neatly into slots, are clearly visible and within easy reach.

(above and left) **When kids can see and reach** where things go, putting clothes and toys away seems more like play. Adjustable shelves and rods are combined with removable and pull-out wire bins to create a convenient closet storage system that more than doubles the space in this child's closet.

Design
Types of Storage

To select the system that's best for you, it's a good idea to familiarize yourself with the various types of storage and storage components available. Adjustable, fixed, open and customized are some of the most common types of storage. And pegs, hooks, racks, shelves, boxes, bins and cabinets are some of the storage components that are used in them. Knowing the specific characteristics of each system will help you decide which types of storage will work best for you and which components to include as part of that system.

Adjustable storage with components like shelves, drawers and bins can be reconfigured into various combinations. This type of system accommodates many items of different shapes and sizes. Stationary storage systems have components, such as shelves and drawers, that are housed in a permanent casing or frame. In some stationary units, the shelves and drawers may be adjustable, in others, components like shelves and drawers are permanently in place. These units are usually stronger and can hold more weight than adjustable storage.

Fixed storage can be built in, attached to the wall or built to fit a specific space. It can also be freestanding. Freestanding storage is often movable storage. This type of storage includes movable furniture and containers such as chests, armoires or rolling kitchen carts. Open storage is one of the simplest forms of storage. It allows quick access to frequently used items.

Item-specific and customized storage are types of systems that have unique and specific characteristics for each situation. Customized storage can be any type of storage specifically created for a special space or to match a certain interior or architectural design theme. Item-specific storage is created to store one specific item, such as a tray designed to hold silverware or a CD holder. You can buy or build a storage system that includes any or all of these types of storage.

(above) **This glass-front china hutch** *is a freestanding storage unit that becomes a beautiful display case for the good china when it's being stored.*

(below) **Pull-out pantry shelves** *allow you to see and reach items easily.*

Commercial storage products are an easy and convenient solution for most of your everyday storage needs. A variety of storage options is available in your local retail stores. Many commercial systems can be mixed and matched to accommodate your specific storage situation. Shelves, racks, crates and bins can be used to accommodate items of all shapes and sizes. Make sure the materials used by the system you choose are strong enough to support the items you wish to store.

(left) **Open shelves, pull-out drawers and fixed cupboards** *are components that were used to create a comfortable amount of storage space in this Euro-style bathroom.*

This contemporary wall unit *features inset shelving with tambour doors that slide closed to protect a media center. This enclosed space is available with item-specific storage units for tapes and CDs. The rest of the unit is fitted with stationary, open shelving, which displays a variety of books and pieces of art.*

13

ADJUSTABLE

Adjustable storage increases the flexibility of a storage system. Whether they are attached to a freestanding cabinet or mounted in a closet, adjustable storage components can be easily rearranged or reconfigured to fit your changing storage needs. Adjustable storage can be used to solve almost any space-planning problem. Shelves that are adjustable in height allow you to store items of different sizes. This type of storage can also be converted to accommodate other components, such as drawers or hanging baskets.

Adjustable storage can be store-bought or custom-built. One of the most common kinds of adjustable storage is called a track system. This type of system is composed of tracks and brackets or tracks and clips. Generally, bracket systems are hung on a wall and clips are used within a cabinet frame or other enclosed area. Tracks should be fastened to wall studs, if possible, especially if they will be used to hold a lot of weight. Look for quality construction and durable materials; poor quality will cause the unit to not fit well or become unsteady.

Photo courtesy of Lee Rowan

Adjustable wire components *increase the storage capabilities throughout your closet. This ventilated wire storage system gives you maximum visibility of your stored items. Wire shelving, sliding drawers, door and wall racks, shoe racks and other adjustable storage accessories are all available from a variety of storage system manufacturers.*

(above) **This multipiece storage system** *is adjustable and versatile. Separate components like a wall-mounted closet, a corner closet, drawers, stackable shoe racks and adjustable shelving can be mixed and matched to fit your personal storage needs.*

(left) **Adjustable racks and shelves** *easily adapt as your storage needs change.*

15

STATIONARY

In a stationary storage system the components cannot be adjusted or changed, so your flexibility is limited. The components of stationary storage, like shelves or doors, may swing or pull out, but they cannot be repositioned within the unit. A stationary storage unit can include a combination of different types of storage, such as pull-out or open storage. Or, a stationary storage unit may simply be a bookcase with fixed shelves that stay permanently in place.

Stationary storage systems often include shallow shelves that are very sturdy. They are an excellent choice for storing heavier, more substantial items such as books or electronic equipment. Stationary shelves are also a better choice for storing fragile or breakable items such as pottery or glassware.

Stationary storage systems are sometimes more aesthetically pleasing and offer more space per inch because no hardware or adjustable mechanisms detract from the clean line of the unit.

*This **built-in bookcase and window seat** are excellent examples of stationary and fixed storage. The bookcase has a stationary frame that cannot be changed, but inside, the shelves are adjustable. The window seat is a stationary unit with all elements permanently fixed.*

*A **contemporary wall unit** uses fixed shelves to hold the weight of this literary collection. An inset cabinet has doors that swing out, then slide into the unit, and out of sight. The open, clean look of the shelving creates a handsome display case for glassware and art objects.*

Sturdy stationary shelves *and deep pull-out drawers handle heavy storage items like the good china and glassware often stored in a formal dining area.*

This detailed storage cabinet was built to fit into an alcove of this dining room wall. The unit includes several types of storage to accommodate a variety of different items. A decorative dish rack and glass-front cupboards turn stored dishes and glassware into a beautiful display.

Types of storage

BUILT-TO-FIT

Built-to-fit storage should not to be confused with built-in, which includes any storage unit that attaches to the wall. Built-to-fit is the cheapest way to get maximum storage use in a specific space. These systems can be set into an alcove, attached to the wall or freestanding in the space. Built-in units of this type are more stable than those that are freestanding. This type of storage system adds personality and a finished look to a room.

Built-to-fit systems are the most efficient way to approach space planning because they can be custom designed to provide storage in those awkward places where a commercial storage unit won't fit. Storage systems that are built to fit can have any configuration of components—fixed or adjustable, shelves or drawers. It's the way you intend to use the system that will determine which ones you want to include.

Pull-out drawers, built into the kneewall, add storage space but don't take up any more floor space in this small attic bedroom.

(left) ***A secretarial desk*** *was built to fit this kitchen corner. The low desk has a shallow drawer and small writing surface. Above the desk, a shelf with cubbyholes beneath holds reference materials and writing materials.*

(below) ***A small home office area*** *was built to fit the underutilized area beneath these steps. The desk has enough desktop area for a computer to sit on comfortably and includes deep pull-out drawers for storing files and documents.*

(above) **A freestanding baker's rack** *makes an attractive and effective kitchen storage unit. The open racks keep all items visible and accessible.*

(left) **A small, freestanding iron rack** *is a fun and functional addition to this corner of the room. The open shelves are handy holders for games, CDs and books.*

FREESTANDING

Freestanding storage units stand independently and often can be moved from place to place easily. This means that unlike most types of built-in storage, they can be taken to your next home. Freestanding storage includes movable containers, such as crates and baskets, and furniture pieces converted to storage, like chests and armoires. Other examples of freestanding storage systems can include: bookcases, entertainment centers, tables and desks. Tall units may be anchored to the wall for safety and stability, if necessary.

Additional freestanding storage can often be gained from furniture items like trunks and chests, which utilize both the inside space and the area on top. Traditional furniture, such as armoires and highboys, was often designed as freestanding storage for rooms without closets. These freestanding units, traditionally used for storing linens and dishes, can be adapted for many different storage functions.

Photo courtesy of Grange

Photo courtesy of Heritage Custom Kitchens

(above) **This Shaker-style armoire** *functions as freestanding storage and adds an authentic accent to the period styling of this room.*

(left) **A traditional highboy and pantry** *offer freestanding storage that matches the old-fashioned appeal of this country kitchen.*

ITEM-SPECIFIC

This type of storage consists of containers or storage units designed to hold specific items. A CD holder or a man's valet are examples of item-specific storage units. Item-specific storage helps protect the stored items and keeps the space organized.

You can buy item-specific storage or have it custom built. It can be fixed or adjustable, freestanding or stationary—the determining factor of item-specific storage is that it is designed for one specific storage function.

Item-specific storage can also be used to store items other than those it was originally intended for. For example, a swing-arm tie rack can be used to store scarves or necklaces, as well as ties. Keep your other storage needs in mind as you shop for item-specific storage units.

A freestanding valet lets you breeze through your morning routine by having your wardrobe at the ready. A belt and tie can be stored on the stainless pull-outs, and your shirt and jacket stay neat on the sturdy hanger.

A pull-out drawer is designed specifically to store CDs.

Stainless steel hampers *instill order and organization. They are perforated to promote air circulation, making them ideal for storing laundry in the bedroom or bath.*

A CD tower frees up shelf space and gives you instant access to your CDs.

A bath shelf keeps your soap, razor, shampoo and washcloth organized and close at hand. This unit can hang from the shower head or be mounted on the wall.

This set of cooking tools *becomes an attractive display when the stainless steel utensils are stored hanging from a stainless steel rack.*

A pull-out ironing board *handles morning touch-ups easily. The board telescopes to easily unfold from the cabinet drawer.*

A decorative glass rack *that attaches under the cupboard stores and protects fragile stemware by hanging it safely out of harm's way.*

A hanging belt and tie rack *keeps items in order and easily accessible. The rotating tie holders help keep that special tie close at hand.*

A simple insert *turns an empty drawer into a pull-out spice rack. This handy holder stores spice bottles in three angled rows, making the labels easy to read and the bottles easy to reach.*

A man's jewelry box *has two lidded compartments and an ample storage area. A removable tray has five compartments for spare change, keys and credit cards.*

This colorful butler's pantry features a wall of open shelving that supports colorful glazed pottery. More wide, open shelves are found below the countertop alongside extra-wide storage drawers.

(above) **This open wire shelving** *mounts on the wall above the counter and keeps cooking items close to the food prep area.*

(top right) **Stored quilts** *stay neat and folded in this open-front window seat. The open frame turns this window seat into a display for the colorful quilts.*

The open shelves *of this large bookcase help users find books effortlessly by displaying the entire collection at once. The adjustable shelves can be moved to accommodate items of various sizes.*

Types of storage

OPEN

Open storage units display their contents for public viewing. These types of storage units can be freestanding or built in. Some of the most common examples include bookcases and shelves. Open storage also includes a type of storage referred to as display storage. Display storage turns open storage into a decorative display.

The primary benefit of an open storage system is visibility and accessibility. Open storage systems keep items organized and out of the way, but still within easy reach. Shelves are one of the most versatile components in an open storage system, especially adjustable shelves which allow open storage units to accommodate items of a wide variety of shapes and sizes. Open systems are often less expensive to buy or build than a closed system, because they don't feature drawers, doors or costly hardware.

One of the drawbacks is that the items kept in an open storage system are often exposed to potential problems, like ultraviolet light and everyday dirt and dust. The items stored here will receive no privacy, and unless they are kept neat and clean, they will look cluttered.

PULL-OUT

Pull-out storage includes drawers, cabinets, trays and shelves that pull out, lift up or swing out. Pull-out storage makes it easier to see and reach the backs of deep shelves and the dark recesses under counters.

Drawers, trays, shelves or sliding palettes that pull out improve both organization and accessibility. These systems can be bought or custom built. Both are more expensive than units with stationary shelving, but are far more efficient. Pull-outs make it easier to stay organized and to see and reach everything you need.

Pull-outs can be positioned close together and stacked vertically to better utilize the available storage space. This type of storage is not recommended for storing fragile items, unless care is taken to prevent them from shifting when the tray or shelf moves.

Pull-out wire storage baskets *enable you to store more items under the sink and allow you to easily see everything you've stored.*

A pull-out drawer *keeps knives at a handy height. A drawer insert holds knives in place and keeps them sharp.*

This cabinet door slides out *to reveal a deep pull-out drawer. The drawer is just the right size for the grocery bags used for recycling.*

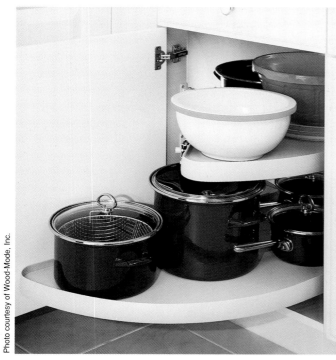

Large items like pots and pans can be easily retrieved from inside deep cabinets with shelves that swing out. The swing-out shelves give you quick access to everything stored.

Space-saving storage bins tilt out to store dishwashing items. These handy bins are shallow enough to take advantage of unused space in cabinets underneath sinks.

Vertical space is utilized by stacking shallow baskets close together. The baskets pull out for easy access.

A pull-out wire clothes bin keeps dirty clothes out of the way until wash day. The open wire construction keeps the air circulating throughout the bin.

Shiny stainless steel and chrome *are used to give the shelves in this customized kitchen corner an ultra-modern appeal. The shallow drawers are ideal for storing flatware, cooking utensils, washcloths and linens. The long handles on the drawers beneath the sink are the perfect place to hang dish towels while they dry.*

Types of storage

CUSTOMIZED

Custom-designed and custom-built storage systems are tailored to fit the dimensions, design and style of your specific space and the items you wish to store. Customized storage offers maximum space utilization, high-quality materials, expert craftsmanship and precise attention to details.

Customized storage is a way to incorporate the different types of storage into one ultimate system designed to meet your specific storage needs. Including as many adjustable features in a customized storage unit as possible increases its efficiency and makes it more functional. For example, including shelves that are adjustable in height means they can be used to store a wider variety of items, while item-specific storage for

items like CDs and tapes can be incorporated to organize and protect valuable property. Because of the many new storage options available today, a customized storage system offers the ultimate in organized storage.

One drawback to a custom storage system is that you don't see the final product, except in drawings, until it is installed. This means you must be very sure about the features, dimensions and overall design of a customized storage unit before it is installed. Moving presents another possible problem if you have customized storage. Often, this type of storage cannot be moved easily and must be dismantled or abandoned if you do move.

(right) **Four separate bins** for recycling are hidden inside a base cabinet. The bins, which are removable for quick recycling, are practical and aesthetically pleasing.

Photos this page courtesy of allmilmö

(above) **These innovative cutlery inserts** are part of an extendible, customized drawer system. They feature individually designed sections for different drawer widths. The dividers are removable for easy cleaning.

(left) **This customized storage system** is extremely efficient, timesaving and attractive. Full extension pull-out drawers are further organized by adding plate racks, lid racks and shelves for anything else that may need special storage requirements.

CUSTOMIZED

This photo and photo bottom left courtesy of Wood-Mode, Inc.

Photo courtesy of Heritage Custom Kitchens

(above) **A spice rack** that has been mounted to the inside of the cabinet door doubles the amount of storage in this kitchen cupboard. Small rails hold the bottled spices on the shelf and keep them organized.

(left) **These custom-made kitchen cabinets** include all kinds of specialty storage. An open dish rack hangs beneath a glass-front cupboard and stores dishes in a delightful display.

(left) **The storage system** in this pantry was specifically designed for the specialty storage needs of food items. Adjustable wire baskets attach to a rack and can be pulled out for better accessibility. Deep pull-out drawers hold dry goods and various linen items.

This multifunctional trolley *is equipped with specialty storage in the form of drawers, pull-out baskets, a large pull-down bin and two deep corner drawers. Glass-front doors close to protect items stored on adjustable shelves. The entire unit is on casters, for mobility, and it is connected with a full lazy Susan, so anything you're searching for spins easily into reach.*

Design
SPECIALTY STORAGE

Often specialty storage is required because of the physical characteristics of the item being stored. Some things, such as food and wine, require very specific conditions to ensure they are properly stored. Temperature, humidity and ventilation are just a few of the factors that specialty storage for these items must be able to control. Specialty storage may also be necessary because of the way an item is used. For example, seasonal items such as jackets and skis are only used at certain times of the year, yet they must be properly stored to ensure their protection until the next use.

Linens and bedding are household items that require specialty storage. Because they aren't used every day, these items should be stored in a system that minimizes wrinkles, either folded flat in a drawer or hanging neatly over a rod. Sports equipment is often used for one season and stored for the rest. This equipment can be damaged by the elements if not stored properly.

Books, documents and photos are very susceptible to damage from light, moisture, heat and insects. Specialty storage in the form of a file cabinet or freestanding secretary are good options for storing these items. Electronic equipment also has special storage requirements. Components should be protected from dust and moisture, and often have special wiring and ventilation requirements that affect storage. Depending on your personal storage needs there are a number of specialty options available from various manufacturers. Researching what's available will help you create a system with components designated for your specialty storage needs.

A handsome wrought-iron stand holds a Project Box which helps you organize the stacks of paper and other miscellaneous items that tend to accumulate on a desk. These special storage units not only save precious desktop space, they can be moved and used anywhere in the house

(left) **With a simple spin** this two-tiered lazy Susan brings stored items from the back of this deep cupboard to the front.

(below) **Delicate dishes** are stored and protected in this decorative dish rack. The individual slots keep the fine china from breaking or chipping.

DISPLAY STORAGE

Display storage is a type of open storage that allows you to include some of your most dramatic, exotic or interesting items in an artistic or aesthetically pleasing display. Display storage is one way to keep a valuable collection safe and organized.

Collections you want to keep in display storage are best kept in the room where they will most likely be used. For example, fine china can be stored and beautifully displayed in a glass-front cabinet in the dining room until its next use. Other ideas for display storage units include: baskets, bookshelves, decorative boxes, plate rails, cup and saucer holders and custom-built shelving or cabinets.

Photo Courtesy of Dania/Chicago, Northwest; Reno; Plummers/Southern California; Scandinavian Designs/Bay Area, Denver

This glass-front cabinet keeps crystal glassware and other delicate art objects safely protected. Adding a spotlight to the inside of the cabinet will create a more dramatic effect and turn this lovely storage piece into a beautiful display case.

Photo courtesy of Cy DeCosse Inc.

Photo courtesy of Crystal Cabinet Works Inc.

(above) A custom-made kitchen cabinet makes a decorative display case for a quaint collection of dishes and teapots.

(left) A simple wooden ladder is an eye-catching and convenient way to store and display decorative dishcloths and towels. Draping the items over the rungs of the ladder keeps them wrinkle-free and within easy reach.

Open shelving and an interesting shape *make this freestanding shelf unit a clever option for many types of display storage. When painted the same deep green color as the pie safe and the chair, it becomes an ideal place to display this delightful collection of decoys.*

(above) **An old-fashioned armoire** is an attractive storage solution for keeping a collection of extra bed linens organized and wrinkle-free.

(right) **Quilts and blankets** can be draped over the rungs of a ladder for convenient storage or as a decorative display. Storing colorful quilts like this can also be a way to accessorize a traditional country motif.

LINENS & BEDDING

The type of storage you use for linens should keep them wrinkle-free. Place mats and napkins can be folded and kept in shallow drawers or on shelves, but tablecloths or bulky blankets are best stored hanging from dowels or slats. This storage method keeps them within easy reach, yet frees valuable shelf space. Hanging linens and blankets also keeps them from getting wrinkled. Rolling the material around large mailing tubes when stored also minimizes wrinkles.

In an existing linen closet, the easiest way to increase your storage space is to add more shelves. Adding a smaller half shelf for hand towels or napkins can usually be done without taking away any existing space. Pull-out baskets and wire trays that hang from shelves are other storage solutions for these items.

A large linen closet uses pull-out shelves to bring hard-to-reach items within easy reach. The position of the shelves can be adjusted to accommodate changing storage needs.

This efficient linen closet makes effective use of an underutilized corner. Designed to save space, this corner cabinet takes up little floor space and offers lots of storage.

A small pie safe makes a clever linen closet. The decorative metal door keeps items safely stored and out of sight.

Wall-mounted racks *free up more floor space and keep items safe and secure.*

When storing bikes, *use a rack that will suspend the bikes by the crossbar. These racks are safer and more secure than those that suspend a bike by the wheel.*

Safe storage for sports equipment *can be a problem because of the large sizes or odd shapes of the equipment. This garage utilizes long cupboards with adjustable shelves to store a variety of sports equipment.*

Specialty storage

SPORTS EQUIPMENT

To eliminate unnecessary clutter, store sports equipment that is out of season, and keep out only what you will really need for the current season. Consider organizing items by sport and bulk. Hang large bulky items like skis, bikes, skates and Rollerblades to keep them from getting damaged. To make your storage unit multifunctional, install some compartments small enough to accommodate accessories like kneepads and goggles.

It's not a good idea to store skis in the garage. They should be kept dry to prevent oxidation. You should also turn ski bindings to zero when stored so they don't lose tension. Ski boots should be stored with buckles at medium tension and the boots stuffed with newspaper, if possible.

Most damage that occurs to bikes during storage happens when bikes tip over. A bike rack will prevent such damage. Crossbar bike racks suspend the bike by the frame. They take up more room but are safer than those that suspend the bike by a wheel, because the frame is designed to take the entire weight of the bike. When storing bicycles, store your helmet, gloves, water bottles, and other cycling accessories together. After long-term storage, be sure to lubricate the chain, and tighten and lubricate the brakes as well. Rollerblades should be hung when stored, to keep them dry. Golf clubs and tennis rackets should be kept covered and away from any moisture. Golf club covers keep the club heads clean and protect against rust.

Adjustable storage *accommodates a variety of winter sporting equipment. Skis, ski boots and skates should be stored in a dry area indoors to protect against rust. The components of this functional storage unit can be reconfigured to accommodate an array of odd-size items.*

The open shelves *underneath this kitchen island are ideal for storing large bowls and ripening fruit. A wine rack has been built into one end of the island. The large rack keeps bottled wine safe and out of the way.*

This deep corner cupboard *can hold lots of dry goods. The large lazy Susan spins to make everything accessible.*

A lattice wall *at the end of this island creates handy and attractive storage for bottled wine.*

FOOD & WINE

Special storage conditions must be considered when storing perishable items like food and wine. Pantries with pull-out components such as shelves and drawers offer an efficient way to store boxed and canned goods.

Wine requires special storage conditions, such as a constant temperature and protection from sunlight and vibrations. If you don't have a formal wine cellar, basements and crawl spaces that stay cool are often ideal spots for storing wine.

For good organization and easy access, store boxes and cans on shelves and in drawers or hanging baskets that pull out. For deep shelves, baskets and drawers with short, open or see-through fronts allow you to locate items before pulling them out.

Dry goods like rice, flour and pasta can be stored for a long period of time, but it is best to keep them in sealed containers where the food will stay dry and protected from insects. There are many options available for storing dry goods on the market today—airtight canisters, stackable plastic containers and jars with lids are just a few options available. Item-specific drawer liners, wire or plastic hanging baskets or an old-fashioned bread box are some other options.

*A **customized storage unit** combines swing-out shelves with open shelving to dramatically increase the amount of storage available in this pantry. Two deep pull-out bins are located at the bottom of the pantry for storing vegetables that don't need refrigeration.*

BOOKS, DOCUMENTS & PHOTOS

Temperature and humidity are two elements that need to be carefully controlled when choosing a storage system for perishable paper items, such as books, magazines, documents, financial records, photos and correspondence. Therefore, hot attics and damp, cold basements are not the places to store these types of items. Ideal storage of paper items is a space that is between 60° and 75°F with humidity between 50 and 60%.

Metal file cabinets, such as those used commercially for business, are an efficient and safe way to store important documents and photos. These file cabinets are available in fireproof models as well as a select variety of styles and colors.

A desktop organizer keeps documents and papers organized and at your fingertips. Small pull-out drawers store smaller items like paper clips and stamps.

A small storage chest is an excellent way to store postcards and other personal keepsakes and mementos. A wooden tray resting on a lip at the top of the trunk utilizes available space by creating a compartment for smaller items that might otherwise get lost.

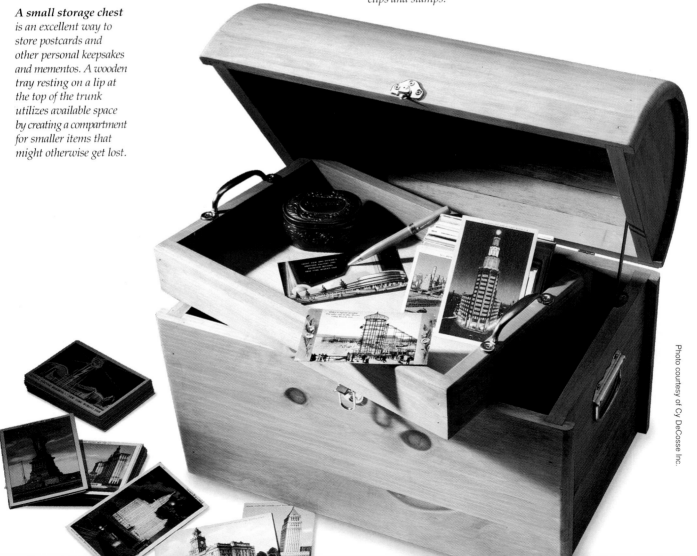

Storage for small objects *is taken care of by this tower of drawers. The shallow drawers help keep desktop items orderly and organized.*

This magazine table *keeps items neatly stacked and ready to read. The four compartments were designed large enough to hold magazines and newspapers and are angled to make it easy to keep everything neat.*

Modular wooden file cabinets *offer beauty and flexibility in a filing system. The drawers are made in sections, so you can buy just the number you need now and add more later. Each drawer is deep enough for hanging files, and locking the drawer in the top position secures all the others beneath it.*

Electronic equipment is properly stored and protected in this contemporary wall unit. Glass-front doors keep items in sight and within easy reach.

A sturdy, space-saving stand has a high platform and swivel base so you can position the television anywhere you desire for optimum viewing.

Specialty storage

ELECTRONIC EQUIPMENT

New technological developments for electronic media equipment such as stereos, CD players, VCRs and personal computers, monitors and printers have introduced a new class of storage needs. Many people choose a freestanding or built-in entertainment center to house their electronic equipment. Entertainment centers improve organization and allow you to store your electronic media in an enclosed and protected space. To make the most efficient use of an entertainment center, measure your TV, stereo and VCR units and configure the shelving to fit. The TV screen should be placed at eye level with the stereo above it, and Nintendo games and other child-oriented components below.

Keep in mind that exposure to dust, sunlight and heat can damage delicate electronics pieces. Storing your electronic equipment in an entertainment center or closed cabinet keeps it protected. if you do choose to put you electronic equipment in a storage unit, be sure to allow enough space for air to circulate around the components and keep them from overheating.

Organizing inserts *make pull-out shelves twice as effective for storing cassette tapes and CDs.*

Organize your media *with a small compartmentalized box like the one shown here. The compartments and drawers are just large enough for CDs and tapes, and the entire unit is compact and portable.*

A rotating CD platform *is uniquely designed to display CDs in individual slots for quick access.*

A space-saving corner cabinet *makes a handy workstation. The cabinet houses a computer and an overhead shelf holds reference materials.*

(above) **Wall-mounted, ventilated steel shelving** keeps gardening tools and potting items dry and out of the way until planting season.

(left) **Attachable components** help store and organize odd-shaped or hard-to-handle items, like garden hoses and electrical cords.

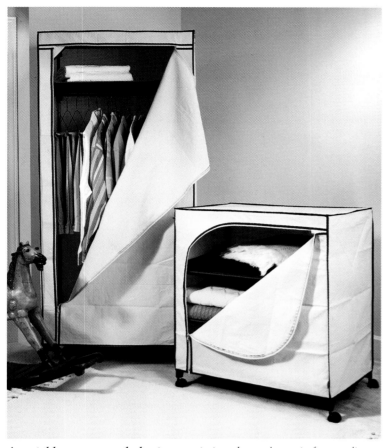

A portable canvas wardrobe stores, protects and organizes out-of-season items. Cotton is a better choice than vinyl, which tears easily and promotes musty odors.

Durable weatherproof covers protect outdoor furniture from the destructive effects of the elements. Covers preserve your furniture's appearance and ensure clean, dry seating and dining surfaces after a storm. Covers with ties and elastic edges stay securely in place during rough weather.

SEASONAL

Items that are used less than once a month or only during a few months out of the year should be put away in a seasonal storage unit. Items that you might consider for seasonal storage include: winter outerwear, like coats and ski pants; sporting goods and athletic equipment, such as ice skates or skis; outdoor furniture and gardening tools.

Portable closets and durable garment bags come in many shapes and sizes, and are effective storage units for seasonal clothing items. Seasonal sporting equipment, such as skis and ice skates, should be stored indoors, because it is susceptible to damage from moisture and extreme temperatures. There are special caddies available to store a number of types of sporting equipment. These storage caddies attach to the wall or hang from the ceiling and hold the stored item securely in place, off the floor and out of the way.

Lawn furniture and gardening tools can be stored in the basement, an outdoor shed or in the garage. Garage and outdoor temperature extremes reduce chances of seed germination and hasten deterioration, so it's best not to keep seeds with yard supplies. Instead, keep seeds indoors and out of the sunlight, in labeled canning jars or other airtight containers.

A PORTFOLIO OF

STORAGE IDEAS

CLOSET & PANTRY STORAGE

Until recently, closets and pantries have been thought of as simple, vertical boxes with rods for hanging clothes or shelves for storing food. These old-fashioned units are rapidly being replaced by storage systems that are more versatile, stylish and imaginative than ever before. Closets and pantries are larger today than in the past, and people are storing more in them. Luckily, innovative new systems are now available with shelves, drawers and racks for specialty items.

These new systems make the most of vertical space by positioning the top rods and shelves a foot higher than traditional closets, creating more room below for additional shelves and rods. Pantry systems are incorporating more pull-out and rotating designs to maximize space.

Organizing your space this way can double the amount of storage space found in a traditional closet or pantry. With a manufactured storage system you can add sections as needed and easily refigure your existing storage whenever you want. Unlike most homemade shelving systems, manufactured storage systems give you the flexibility to incorporate additional components, such as shelves, drawers and baskets.

Consider the flexibility of a system before you buy it. Does it have the right configuration of rods, shelves and other accessories? Can you rearrange it or move it as needed? Buying a manufactured system allows you to purchase additional components and easily adapt to your changing budget and storage needs.

This walk-in closet *features extra racks for specialty items like shoes and ties, creating more space along the floor for a second hanger rack.*

(right) **Separate storage bins** *for white and dark laundry make sorting dirty clothes easy.*

(far right) **Wire handles** *add a decorative touch to these closet drawers.*

(right) **Shallow drawers** *with see-through acrylic fronts allow you to identify your clothes at a glance.*

(far right) **These long slide-out** *drawers keep shirts organized and neat.*

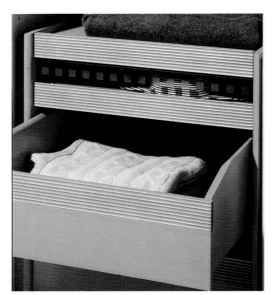

(right) **A tie rack can be fitted** *in any small closet space.*

(far right) **These deep bins allow** *you to store a large volume of clothing in contemporary style.*

The traditional above-the-rack shelf is still a great way to store seldom-used items.

The function of a bedroom closet is to store and maintain clothes. One way to start organizing is to make a list of what needs to be hung, folded and easily accessed. Keep elements together in designated categories such as style, color or fabric. You can also categorize clothes by how you use them, dividing your wardrobe into work and casual sections.

Hanging clothing by length makes good use of space. Clothes should be double-hung whenever possible, and full-length items should hang at eye level. Pay attention to fabric types. Knits, for instance, should be kept folded and flat.

The best way to store accessories is to apply the three basic components of storage—hook, container or shelf. Boxes can customize drawers and shelves by holding items of many sizes, as long as the items of the same size are stored together. And don't forget the back of the door, the most overlooked part of the closet. The back of a closet door is perfect for shoe trees, belt hooks or tie racks.

To get the most out of your storage space, *consider combining compartments for flexibility. This closet meshes simple box shelves, hanging rods and drawers for an efficient and versatile storage system.*

Traditionally a pantry was a small room situated in the passageway between the kitchen and the dining room. Today a pantry can be a separate room, a freestanding cabinet or a set of open shelves. Whatever the design, a pantry allows the whole kitchen to function more efficiently. A well-designed pantry should have a large capacity and allow you to view its contents at a glance.

The goals of pantry organization are visibility and accessibility. Pull-out and rotating shelves aid accessibility, while adjustable shelves allow you to reconfigure your pantry as your needs change and grow.

(above) ***Even a small kitchen pantry*** *can be invaluable as storage space. This well-organized pantry stores everything from cleaning detergent to food supplies.*

(left) ***An extensive walk-in pantry*** *makes life easy in the kitchen. The open shelving system allows you to spot needed items in a flash.*

The vinyl-coated wire shelves add style to this exposed pantry. Exposed storage can be a decorative feature of a kitchen, and it forces you to keep your items organized.

KITCHEN STORAGE

Food storage and meal preparation are the primary functions of your kitchen. To increase the efficiency of the room, store your most commonly used kitchen tools where they will be used most frequently. Items that are used every day should be positioned between shoulder and hip height to minimize bending and stretching.

Add space by getting rid of the unused gadgets that always seem to accumulate in a kitchen. You can store items on walls, hooks, pegboards or wire grids. Pots and pans can be suspended from the ceiling or a wall rack for easy accessibility. Like cooking mitts and baskets, pots and pans provide a decorative function as well as a useful one when you hang them on the wall.

The area on top of and above the counter is the most accessible in the room. Use this space wisely by filling it with functional storage, such as a knife rack or wall-mounted appliances. High shelves are good places to store seldom-used items like decorative dishes, vases and large pots and pans.

There are a number of innovative new products you can buy to make it easy to organize your kitchen. In-drawer or on-shelf organizers keep small items in place and within easy reach. Under-shelf or under-cabinet organizers and bins hang on the inside of cabinet doors to hold items securely in place and within easy view. Turntables for cabinets and pantries provide easy access to deep storage areas, and rolling kitchen carts fill wasted space in corners and under windows with practical, mobile storage.

A traditional kitchen storage system is improved with the addition of a few exposed shelf areas for convenient access to kitchen items.

Decorative display storage in the form of glass-front cupboards, a built-in dish rack and hooks for hanging cups and towels is combined with pull-out drawers and closed cabinets to create an effective and attractive kitchen storage system.

Photos both pages courtesy of KraftMaid Cabinetry, Inc.

It's difficult to have too much storage in a kitchen. In the absence of a pantry, this kitchen fills nearly all the unused space with cupboards and drawers.

Many modern kitchens contain a central workstation *for food preparation and storage. The central workstation featured above is basically a storage unit with a top work surface attached.*

An efficient kitchen takes advantage of even small spaces. This tiny nook stores everything needed for a morning breakfast.

Large photo courtesy of KraftMaid Cabinetry, Inc., inset photo courtesy of Wood-Mode, Inc.

Don't forget that kitchen storage *includes displaying decorative touches on the counter space and above the cupboards.*

Tall cupboards support *a kitchen worksurface. With the addition of a few chairs, this extended storage unit and surface becomes a modern type of kitchen table.*

Exposed shelves, *rolltop compartments, a wine rack and traditional covered shelves mesh within one large bank of cupboards.*

BATHROOM STORAGE

Like a kitchen, a bathroom should be organized for maximum efficiency. You should never have to leave the room to get something you use regularly, and everything you need should be within easy reach.

A well-organized bathroom should have easily accessible storage for towels, paper products and robes. It should also have storage for toiletries and cleaning supplies, as well as a separate space for small electronic items like hair dryers and curling irons. A safe, separate storage area for medicine and other personal hygiene items is also useful.

Some ideas for saving space in the bathroom include customized drawers and pull-out trays.

You can customize a drawer by using inserts to divide the drawer into smaller sections specifically designed for your possessions. You can also keep everyday items handy but contained by using baskets, trays, plastic storage bins or caddies.

Shower caddies hang from a shower head or attach to a corner of the tub for holding shampoo, soap and washcloths. You also can find caddies to hold electrical appliances like hair dryers and curling irons. These caddies can sit on a countertop or be attached to a wall. Small containers like vinyl-coated baskets are available to hold items of varying sizes and are generally a good way to reduce bathroom clutter and mess.

Featuring ample storage space *above and below the sink and an over-the-tub storage compartment, this bathroom has all the space you would need to keep your bathroom items in order.*

Photo courtesy of KraftMaid Cabinetry, Inc.

Photo right courtesy of Crystal Cabinet Works Inc., inset photo courtesy of Frontgate® Catalog

In addition to the standard cabinets *above and below the sink, this bathroom contains an open unit attached to the wall for easy access to perfume, lotions and cologne.*

(above) **An open cabinet** on the wall transforms bathing oils into attractive decorative items. *(inset)* **An attractive clothes hamper** is always a great choice for keeping your laundry stored in style.

This centrally located cabinet has a glass door, making it easy to locate needed items at a glance.

(left) **A cloth sink apron** *drapes the basin to create a handy and attractive storage space in an unused area.*

(below) **Sometimes just a small area** *will suffice. This bathroom features a small wooden stand for towel storage. Behind the tub is another small stand for toiletry articles.*

This fully stocked bathroom *contains a floor-to-ceiling storage space in addition to the standard cabinetry. Simple options like this make it easy to store all your bathroom articles.*

(left) **Solid units** of hardwood cabinets divide the storage into convenient compartments and help to define the look of the entire bathroom.

(below) **A tall cabinet** in the center of the sink area helps to define the space and separate the two mirror stations while providing plenty of storage for the room.

BEDROOM STORAGE

Bedrooms have more than one function—they are places where we read, listen to music, watch television, dress and sleep. To accommodate all these activities and the special storage needs of clothing and accessory items, bedroom storage systems must be more complex and less obtrusive than other storage systems. To fulfill the storage requirements in your bedroom, you can choose the informal look of simple bins or baskets, or the traditional approach of wooden furniture and closed cabinets. Whatever style you choose, efficiency and good organization are the goals.

Customized and built-to-fit units are good choices for bedroom storage; they can store hanging and folded garments of all shapes and sizes, as well as jewelry, shoes and other accessories. The advantage of a customized or built-to-fit storage system for the bedroom is that it makes excellent use of space and can be built to match your decor and perfectly fit your space. Unfortunately, these units can be expensive, and you often can't take them with you if you move.

Underutilized storage space can often be found under the bed. There are ready-made boxes and containers that slide under a standard bed frame. Tray and chests specifically made for underbed storage are available in plastic, wood or cardboard. These inexpensive storage containers are perfect for storing seasonal clothing.

Consider headboards and custom bed frames with convenient built-in bedside storage. Bedroom wall storage systems are another popular way to keep all bedroom items close at hand, but out of sight.

This tiny closet contains a single rack for hanging clothes and a series of shelves for boxes to fill some modest storage needs.

This bedroom combines the best of modern storage. One section of the room features a wall of exposed shelving, the other has a tightly packed, unobtrusive closet.

Photos both pages courtesy of interlübke

A bedroom closet should feature *a combination of shelving and racks. With these sections divided, you make the most efficient use of your space.*

In addition to providing storage, *these fashionable cabinets set the tone of the bedroom.*

This closet unit combines several types of storage *to create a unified scheme of convenient bedroom organization. The raised central rack gives the owner more room for shelving. The shoe shelf is raised from the floor to eliminate bending.*

Two large, mirrored armoires *frame the fireplace and provide all the storage this bedroom needs, while creating an optical illusion of increased space.*

A traditional bedroom set, with contemporary styling, features a nightstand, a double dresser, an armoire and a 7-drawer chest for ample bedroom storage.

Photos both pages courtesy of Dania/Chicago, Northwest, Reno; Plummers/Southern California; Scandinavian Designs/Bay Area, Denver

*A **teen's bedroom collection** includes a large trundle-like storage drawer that pulls out from under the bed. A nightstand on casters and a 5-drawer chest provide storage for clothing items while a desk with file drawers is a great place to store schoolwork.*

***This contemporary youth's bedroom** includes a full range of storage options. Large under-bed drawers hold extra quilts and blankets. A bookcase headboard is a handy place for books and favorite photos. A 3-drawer and a 5-drawer chest offer plenty of storage for clothing. And a desk with a hutch and a large bookcase provide storage for a study area in the corner.*

HOME OFFICE & STUDY STORAGE

Many homes have a room designated as an office. Whether you are performing simple home bookkeeping or professional tasks, you will need to deal with space restrictions and organize your storage areas to accommodate your working needs. Plan the space so it functions best for the tasks you need to perform.

Your workstations dictate storage location. Even if you are sharing a desk, it should be large enough to accommodate a computer and its components. Configure your workstation and desk so that everything you need to conduct business is close at hand. Make sure you don't

have to leave the desk for supplies or equipment.

You will need some kind of storage to protect computer disks, documents and other valuable office and study items from sunlight and temperature extremes. Remember, magnetic fields around any electrical device can demagnetize your floppy disks. Mobile files that roll underneath a desk and storage cabinets that fit above it are convenient and easily accessible. An old hutch can be used to hold office supplies and flat items such as artwork. Freestanding adjustable storage units are extremely versatile and are a good option for any home office.

Vinyl-coated wire shelves *provide efficient storage for this home work center. The mobile cart fits under the lower shelf to increase the storage space and improve organization. The entire work area fits into a closet area to be hidden behind closed doors when not in use.*

Modular wall components *make up this multifunctional unit. Curio cabinets feature soft lighting and glass doors. Closed cabinets and shallow drawers offer more storage for those items you wish to keep out of sight.*

(below) **This home theater** storage unit has room for a 35" television as well as plenty of storage for all components and accessories.

This home office *features several separate components that can be mixed and matched to an arrangement that works best for you. Some of the storage components used include a 3-drawer file cabinet, a low bookcase and a medium bookcase, a storage cabinet with door and drawers and a tall hutch.*

Photo courtesy of Levenger

(left) *A bookshelf* on the wall stores volumes of useful office material, while the items needed every day are kept close in this desk-top organizer.

(below) *This home office* has storage designed to grow with your changing needs. The computer table has a pull-out shelf that keeps a computer key pad safely under the desk, but ready whenever you are. A mobile file cabinet, a large corner bookshelf, and a lateral file are other storage units that make up this efficient office space.

This photo and photo bottom right courtesy of Dania/Chicago, Northwest, Reno; Plummers/Southern California; Scandinavian Designs/Bay Area, Denver *(right)* **The dark color** tones in this large cabinet lend a traditional feel to the office. These types of large, imposing units were once the office standards, and are still quite popular.

(bottom) **This modern** study features a large storage cabinet for books, sculpture and audio-visual material. Unlike some earlier generations of office furniture, these modern storage units can be fairly large without exuding the traditional Old World overtones.

Photo courtesy of Eagle Window & Door

Photo courtesy of Wellington Hall, Ltd

Photo Courtesy of Dania/Chicago, Northwest, Reno; Plummers/Southern California; Scandinavian Designs/Bay Area, Denver

This attractive traditional storage unit *can be used as decorative or display storage, as well as a wall unit for an entertainment center. The unit features open shelves and closed cupboards for convenient storage options.*

BASEMENT, ATTIC & GARAGE STORAGE

Make more storage space in your everyday closets by storing seasonal or seldom-worn clothing and other items in a portable closet in the basement, attic or garage. Basements, attics and garages are the catch-all for most of our seasonal and extraneous storage. You can greatly increase the storage capacity of any of these spaces by adding shelves, bins, racks or hooks. Storing items in lofts frees floor space below. Commercial fold-down stairs offer easy access to objects stored above.

Wall racks are great for organizing garden tools, folding lawn furniture and sports equipment. When storing tools, try to hang small items on a wall in order to leave room on the floor for large pieces of equipment. A pegboard can be fitted with various hooks and hangers for storing tools. Bicycles can also be stored on heavy hooks that attach to the wall or hang from ceiling joists.

Holiday decorations and other fragile items should be stored in some type of closed storage, such as boxes, crates or bins to protect them from dust and moisture.

Large, open closets are good for storing seasonal clothing, garden and house maintenance tools, cleaning supplies and firewood. Harmful substances should be stacked in airtight containers on high shelves, or locked in a storage cabinet, away from small children and pets.

This basic shelf system *makes the perfect utility area. Separate compartments keep the tools and supplies organized, and a small entertainment center is built in to keep simple chores interesting.*

Garage storage is clean and organized with this homemade shelving unit. With the notches along the beams, the owners can adjust the shelves or add some more as needed.

(left) **The advantage** to homemade shelving is that you can build it to match your storage needs.

(below) **Retail purchased vinyl-coated wire shelving** is adjustable and portable. It's always a great choice for a basement, attic or garage.

(right) **Basement storage is very** important because of space restrictions. This multishelf unit keeps the items stored neatly and conveniently.

(right) **It's usually best** to store your laundry supplies above or alongside the washer and dryer.

This photo and photo below courtesy of Cy DeCosse Inc.

Photo courtesy of ClosetMaid®

A long row of vinyl-coated wire shelving makes it easy to store your laundry supplies and hang your delicate washables.

Organized storage *should be of primary importance in a shop area. Your projects are completed faster when you know where to find your equipment, and the safety level increases mightily.*

Store seasonal or seldom-used items in the basement. Keep the areas neat and clean for easy retrieval.

Photo courtesy of Knape & Vogt Manufacturing Co.

This photo and photo opposite page courtesy of Cy DeCosse Inc.

Wall racks such as this are perfect for organizing and storing tools you need at your fingertips.

LIST OF CONTRIBUTORS

We'd like to thank the following companies for providing the photographs used in this book:

allmilmö Corporation
70 Clinton Rd.
Fairfield, NJ 07004
(201) 227-2502

Broyhill Furniture Industries, Inc.
One Broyhill Park
Lenoir, NC 28633
(704) 758-3111

Bruce Hardwood Floors
A Division of Triangle Pacific Corp.
16803 Dallas Parkway
Dallas, TX 75428
(800) 526-0308

California Closets
1700 Montgomery Street, Suite 249
San Francisco, CA 94111
1-800-2SIMPLIFY

ClosetMaid®
720 Southwest 17th Street
Ocala, FL 34478
(904) 351-6108

Crystal Cabinet Works, Inc.
1100 Crystal Drive
Princeton, MN 55371
(612) 389-4187

Dania/Chicago
1001 Skokie Blvd.
Northbrook, IL 60062
(708) 205-9910

Dania/Northwest
5920 South 180th Street
Tukwila, WA 98188
(206) 575-1930

Dania/Reno
2580 Kietzke Lane
Reno, NV 89502
(702) 828-4050

Eagle Window & Door Inc.
375 East 9th, P.O. Box 1072
Dubuque, IA 52004-1072
(319) 556-2270

Frontgate
Cinmar, L.P.
2800 Henkle Drive
Lebanon, OH 45036
(800) 626-6488

GenCorp Wallcovering Division
Three University Plaza
Hackensack, NJ 07601
(201) 489-0100

Grange
200 Lexington Avenue
New York, NY 10016
1-800-GRANGE-1

Heritage Custom Kitchens
215 Diller Avenue
New Holland, PA 17557
(717) 354-4011

interlübke
P.O. Box 139
Athens, NY 12015
(518) 945-1007

Knape & Vogt Manufacturing Company
2700 Oak Industrial Drive N.E.
Grand Rapids, MI 49505
(616) 459-3311

KraftMaid Cabinetry, Inc.
16052 Industrial Parkway
P.O. Box 1055
Middlefield, OH 44062
(800) 442-1986
http:\\www.kraftmaid.com

Laura Ashley
(800) 367-2000

Lee Rowan Co.
900 South Highway Drive
Fenton, MO 63026
(314) 343-0700

Levenger
420 Commerce Drive
Delray Beach, FL 33445-4696
(800) 544-0880
levenger@gate.net

Merillat Industries, Inc.
P.O. Box 1946
Adrian, MI 49221-1946
(800) 624-1250

Plummers/Southern California
8876 Venice Blvd.
West Los Angeles, CA 90034
(310) 837-0138

Scandinavian Designs/
Bay Area, Denver
3480 Industrial Drive
Santa Rosa, CA 95403
(707) 528-6640

Springs Window Fashions
7549 Graber Road
Middleton, WI 53562-1096

Stanley Home Decor
480 Myrtle Street
New Britain, CT 06053
(203) 827-5724

Timberpeg
P.O. Box 5474
West Lebanon, NH 03784
(603) 298-8820

Wellington Hall, Ltd.
P.O. Box 1354
Lexington, NC 27293
(704) 249-4931

Wood-Mode, Inc.
1 Second Street
Kreamer PA 17833
(717) 374-2711